becoming
broken

becoming
broken

MASADA JONES

BOOTSTRAP PRESS / FREEVERSE!
2016

LOWELL
MASSACHUSETTS

Typesetting & book design by Ryan Gallagher.
Cover design by Isaiah Stephens.
Author photo by Tory Germann.

Bootstrap Press

East Coast:

31 Wyman Street
Lowell, MA 01852

West Coast:

365 Euclid Ave #107
Oakland, CA 94610

Bootstrap Press books are designed
and edited by Derek Fenner and
Ryan Gallagher.

www.bootstrappress.org/

*This book was made
possible because of Lowell's
Local Cultural Council of
Massachusetts. Funding
for this project will allow
FreeVerse! to sell books to
continue to sustain their
mission of serving youth
in Lowell, as well as draw
attention to the artistic
talents in the city.*

massculturalcouncil.org

This book is dedicated to my family:

Attle, Benjamin, Andre, and Diamond

&

To all who I love past, present, and future.

Lisa,
Thank you so much
for the support!
♡ mjones   6 | 2020

becom
becomin
broken
broken

becoming broken

MASADA JONES

may you walk ever
loved and in love
know the sun
for warmth the moon
for direction
may these words always
remind you your breath
is sacred words
bring out the god
in you

Suheir Hammad

Andre
      my baby
            she screamed in the backyard

Knew I should have stayed home

Instead I walked to work in the rain
Wearing the Jordans he bought me

    Crying in bed
    Silently praying that it was a different time
    Head pounding
    Eyes
    Waterfalls
    Cry
    Remember him taunting me
    Cry   baby cry
    And I would sound like a fire truck
    Hoping my tears and cries would make him stop
    Now I'm crying for him

Andre
my baby she cries
Hear her through my window

Each time I hear his name
Knowing I will never see him
I lose bits of my soul
I'm losing it
I knew I should have stayed home
Instead I walked to work
Wearing the Jordans he bought me
Masada
There's a call parked to you
My co-worker tells me

My baby

I think they killed my baby

My mother screamed

My brother is no longer here

I never want to see a mother cry
                    the way my mother cried

Andre my baby she screams

She proudly acknowledges *I was 15 when I had him*

They were more like brother and sister
They grew up together

Wish

You could have seen them

*

After he passed brave
Face we put on for the world

Do not ask
            if
                I'm fine

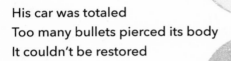

His car was totaled
Too many bullets pierced its body
It couldn't be restored

Did you think twice
Before you put key to ignition?

There are bullets flying hungry for your flesh
You don't realize the one that has bitten your leg
You put key to ignition
        Gas pedal down
        You have got to move faster than
                these bullets
You don't realize what you left behind
But I do
She's six months pregnant
        Ya know
                Carries my nephew in her womb
        My brother didn't come home last night
        She tells my mother she thinks he's cheating

I just want to protect him
Tell her   Ma
Tell her

That he stayed with us and he's sleeping

I didn't know
He'd sleep forever

You don't realize what you left behind
But I do
There was no 911 call for my brother
You left him for dead
Hear you still call him your friend
       You left him for dead

She was six months pregnant
My nephew is now eight
He looks just like him
One day he will ask more questions

My heart is
    52
      pick up

Pray
I have more than 52 answers
When that day comes

You can't empathize with me

When I finally saw you
Wanted you to look broken
Like dreams my brother had
Of teaching my nephew how to play basketball
Like my mother's heart
But you stood tall and proud
Like the cross that hung
At my brother's funeral
You leaned on a fence
Holding a cup of beer
I'm holding the Take Back the Night banner
Can't keep my eyes off you
I'm marching
Protesting violence
All I can think about is hurting you
This march is an oxymoron
I'm the leader
Where do I go from here
My feet mimic cement
Just want you to feel our pain
The scarlet letters of coward are not enough
Too often
They are mistaken for warrior paint
You say you loved my brother
There is no sympathy in that statement
There are smirks in the crevices of your smile

Malice in your eyes

His passing feels like yesterday
Hear you walk like it's been two decades
Sympathy never regarded in your face
Did you think twice before you put key to ignition?
Before driving yourself to the hospital
　　　You left him

　　　Your blood
Messy
In his driver's seat
　　　You left him for dead
His car keys jingling in your hand
　　　Your heart is all icebergs
Cold in your eyes
There's no hope for people like you
His key chain
Imprinted in your palm
Gripping it
Dodging bullets
Holding on to what held your tomorrow
　　　I just wish
　　　　　I just wish

It was my brother's hand

As I write God is
Bowling thunder erupts thoughts
So small we all are

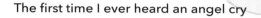

The first time I ever heard an angel cry

Sat by my window wondering why it was
only raining on my house

Her tears
Splattering on my rooftop
Eyes swollen and red

Watched in my kitchen my mother's usual smile
Robbed by pain
Her sobs
The language
Only mothers know

Her warrior
Shot down in our hometown
She said
She should've let him join the army
A battlefield
Shouldn't hit this close to home
Over there
Is over here now
Outside our home everyone is a potential enemy

My mother's heart was once beautiful
Now it's coated by the same dirt that buries her son

I'm convinced she forgets
She has two daughters that love her
We just want to make her proud

There are still tears in my throat
Crying to be heard
Held in limbo
My voice is dust
Barely held together by the fear of honesty

My mother's mouth
Is all delicate razor
Sharp-tongued and orchid-lipped

There are flowers trying to sprout
                out of her soiled heart

                She won't let the light shine through

They are budding
Moistened by countless nights of endless tear-baths
She has the potential to be rose
Her son

My brother
Stemmed deep in her roots
Would never want her to forget him
Just bloom
So her other children can plant root in her shade
He's stimulating her growth
Bulbs are vining in her throat
Ma
Magically maneuver more than wishes
                        through that backbone

Hope has not forgotten you
You've forgotten faith
Used to listen in my bedroom
Mouthing with you
The Lord is my Shepherd
Once knew it verbatim
There are holes in the psalms now
No truth in any prayer
You prayed for him religiously
Religion let you down

You are more than wilted rose
More than tainted petals of he-loves-me-nots
This is not just about God

We want you to seep into beautiful
                    stone and fortress

There will be light
Promise me you will bask
        Glow
You are not clouded shadows
        Ma
Your son wants you to live

Can you forever stay his memory?

Remember we are here and we love you

Let's pray for old time sake

The Lord is my Shepherd I shall not want
He makes me to lie down in green pastures
He lies me beside still waters

This is our prayer
There are emotions you know
That I may never

Ma
If I could live for you
Don't doubt that I would

Five years have passed

This one is a leap year

Your son is your doppelganger
You weigh heavy on my mind
This is the month of your birth

This
The most peculiar winter I've ever witnessed

Almost no snow

It's been five years
The winds whirl wondrously and furious

Windstormed heart reflects the weather

There is no snow

I cannot produce tears in this cold climate

I'm broken

Sometimes there is nothing more for me to do than

Shine

It's winter

Most days it is above average
But at night it is always
The coldest

There is nothing but hurt and
Memories to keep me warm

I miss you

There's nothing like breathing
I inhale exhale and appreciate
Air

Want to hold sun in my mouth
See if my dark cheeks become
Casing for shine
Will I explode if I swallow?
Will my insides glow?
Delight at my grasp is unnatural
There's sun in my room at night
Gleam on my back
I feel it
It is happiness all too often forgotten
Try to embrace the calm
When the storm has decided to settle
In the orchestra of my womb
Clinch tight to the contentment
There's a smile stuck like a hiccup
Unfamiliar in my gasket throat
Enjoy this found freedom
In the showing of teeth
This body is band
Organs all instruments
Find pleasure in me
In me there is instrumental on repeat
My lyric smile
Songbird mounting on my moon lips

Want this song to last forever

Like the first fall wind to knock leaves from trees
The feeling is undeniably beautiful
Here I find me in celibacy of my untouched being
Here I hold on to the me with a smile
Long forgotten the he's who made
These lips turn frown
It is better harvesting love on my own
No one to take it from me when
These hands find comfort
In the palms of others
Somewhere there's a song on low
Playing the same key
Of my body's music

I will find that song one day
One day it will harvest love inside me
Solely because I knew love from me first
Somewhere there is someone
Experiencing this same feeling
Will remember this much more often
Remember that I am not the only
One with a jammed smile
My smile is a forget-me-not letter I wrote to myself
Smile harder when I see it

My body is a temple
A piece of art
Shouldn't be neglected

Sound of sirens frightens me

My body tense
Statuesque whenever one alarms
Swollen throat and panic attack

It took me 5 yrs to get my license
Too worried about what would happen
        if my seatbelt wouldn't unclick

My windows closed me in
                under water
What if fire got me before fighting arms?

I never thought about how his body would lay
Never imagined his motorcycle lying beside him

This man lifeless
Lungs barely succumbing to their will for air

In that moment I prayed he remembered
        how to inhale
Me
I am all shaken and light-headed

Everyone is staring at me
I did nothing wrong
He
Ran the stop sign
Quick victim turned defendant
His motorcycle
My car
Dressed this ground in glitter
I did not find it beautiful
Our fatigued bodies looking up at us in chaos
My legs toddler-unsteady
This rock is home
Plant these feet to the ground
I am not going anywhere
I just need to sit so my head will stop spinning
I am college-student-first-time-drunk
Here
Not alert
But here
There are questions being asked
I hear but am not listening
Officer can you repeat that again
Their stares are so loud
I swear I see a boy mouth the words *her fault*
My eyelids fondle tears
They are screams too afraid to be let loose

I blink
Nod to the officer
His lips continue to move

This street is unfamiliar
My friend lives the next one over

He is at work
He won't know what happened to me today

Won't know that I could've hit the pole
Won't know that my arms felt like jello

He'll ride over our glitter
          and wonder why
                    his cable wasn't working

Naked
Bare brown body lying on this bed
Your chiseled veins
Speaking stories your lips refused to utter
I read them you know
Felt over each scar as you slept
There are secrets you think you have
My body felt them long ago
Begged you to be a man
Don't break what's trying to mend you

Speak truth and let my heart beat
                    to the rhythm of its honesty

You missed bible study the day
                    pastor spoke of love and fear

My only wrong doing
Opening my body
In order for you to heal

Your voice faint
Shaky in places it should be strong

Knew that you were broken
Know that hurt people hurt people
Know that I am whole

Didn't think this timid man of God
                could make me question my stability

How does it feel
To hurt the woman who begged
You to let her love you?

Only asked that when you took breaths
                        you thought of me

Wanted to be a part of something you needed
Let you sleep inside me
Finding comfort in the heat of my womb
Your seed not ready to make a life there
Just hiccup a missed period

How does it feel to revert to silence?
The only thing I know how to use
My voice
Isn't powerful in your game
                of who can be quiet the longest

You don't play fair
Hope that she was worth it

Hope that now every time you take a breath
You think of me
And regret slaps the shit out of you

Oh yeah
        I'll tell you something

I think you'll understand

When I say that something

        I want to hold your hand
        I want to hold your hand
        I want to hold your hand

I sat admiring your profile
            the whole car ride
You took your eyes off the road
            twice
Once to smile at my comment
Second to offer nod of assurance

Both made flowers erupt from my desert womb

My ocean dry for years now
You are my oasis
        I'm almost positive you don't know this

Want you to hold my hand
                        like gear
Shift it to my knee

Show some interest

Be my sea

Leave my desert with more than seashells
                        and starfish
I want more than a revery
                        of you

Want your onyx eyes
            to glance over much
                        more often

I'm not sure
I know how to tell you
Any of this

Yet

Not sure if I ever will

At times
    there is courage
        swimming in thoughts of you

This ocean throat can't gurgle out the words

That you are rainfall
        in drought
            of mid July

                    My deserted heart
Needs the moisture
I know you possess

This car ride
    is magnificent

                Torture
The radio
    is but background
            music to the roaring silence

Want to keep my eyes on the road
    they are glued to your profile
        and the outline of your lips

How would they feel against mine?

Wish my lips would part and spill
                    out these questions

I hold them back
            with clenched teeth
                    and awkward smiles

Wonder if you can see my heart
                    pound against my shirt and jacket?
Are you skeptical of why my hands
            have not left my pockets?

They want nothing more than to twirl
            hope of us onto your scalp

Instead I fight all the urges
Hum whatever tune is on the radio

Don't know the next time I'll have this
Opportunity
I suffer in silence

Making small talk about music and the workplace

We once shared

You don't know that
When I touch you
I feel happy inside

It's such a feeling that my love
I can't hide
I can't hide
I can't gather the courage to tell you

Now my eyes tremble when they close
The anger in your voice magnifies
Baptize
In your spit
No birds chirped
No tune of winged freedom or beauty
You killed goodness in mere minutes
Astounding
How quickly power shifts
How rage takes over

Children
Understand
                    No
You
            You don't care for rules or understanding

Who survives you?
You tornado of a man

I prayed basement

Anything for shelter

Who do you
Pray to?
Where do your wishes travel?
Who do you
Humble yourself before?

My body is not your heaven
Not yours

I was not your
First
Not the first to feel fists

Who did they belong to before they found me?

My face must have felt like home
Your demons unsettling
Refuge in my car
Sat possessively poised
Calm
Gleaming through eye slits
This is you
Your street corner bravado
Found dark alley

Was my strength a threat?

Did you see hoodie and rival colors
Cause my skirt
Did not drop when you said so?

A shame really

Often I recall our first date
How that November day felt like spring

You made butterflies sprout
                          out of cocooned caterpillars
You smiled them into survival
                          we had high hopes

Suppose there's a reason why
          we don't see butterflies in November

Even if it feels like May
Red rage blending beautifully in favoring foliage
Dormant and playing possum
Call me a fool
Call my heart carelessly courageous
Wondering why honesty
Wounds you

Taurus horns on defense
You can be so gentle

First encountered the side
            you show your daughter

Is your darkness always so close by?

Your tormented soul
            a shadow in the sunlight

Is your burden heavy?

My face
        a resting place for the weight of your world

So
I've finally discovered
        that I am worth more

Now I smile
        more
                often that is

                I give birth to poetry

Write words to define me
Who I really am
Mindset is so much different

            from *if he wants to be with me*
            than that means I must be pretty

Now I know I am beautiful
A wise woman once told me I was beautiful
I quickly made it into a joke
        not knowing how to take a compliment
Since all my dudes had told me
        I was cute with a big *butt*
Didn't know my worth

So I thought I was cute with a big butt
Always wanted show my butt
But now I show my mind

I walk head-to-the-sky
        lips-to-microphone
                and hands-on-hips

I've had way too many people look and judge me
Please dare to be different from them
I want to share with you
        the most precious possession I own
My mind
I now own me
Not easily influenced
        by those that want to keep me down

Now two-step on clouds kiss the sun in the morning
        and at night sing the moon a lullaby
Before I leave for school I smother God with hugs

I am a goddess

At one time you used strings to tame me
Was so naïve I let you play me
You were not prepared for me to break free

I am not your zombie
I am very much alive

Nefertiti the beautiful queen of Egypt gave me cpr
With each compression she whispered *fight it sister*
You've got to fight it   I refuse to lose another one

So I did
Awoke and snipped each string that was once
Pulled by them

You no longer own me

Threw away my magazines and no longer watch TV
You cannot make me kill myself in my own mind
                              because I don't look like
                                             them
Sick of hearing *you'd be beautiful if you were skinny*

You have a pretty face
If only you were a few shades lighter

I am beautiful

Media
        who do you think you are?

Hypnotizing these men to the point where they
        don't even know what they want anymore

Wanting girls that look like video vixens

The way you talk
                it's now so condescending

You were never like that in grade school

I know your mother she was my babysitter

She definitely taught you better

Guess the way misogynists use their words
                        are more clever

You want to be just like them

We seem to forget that we both came from Adam

Adam now comes from me
Needed you to be
You need me
        to leave your legacy

But I digress

I once screamed inside my skin

Was dying inside

Can't say I haven't contemplated it

Not suicide
But using bleach peroxides dyes and lye
Broke through

Fell in love
           with the freedom
                    of my afro
                             and the uncontrolled

                    sway of my hips

I am Me

Media
           do something else

                    to jeopardize my image

I dare you

I will scream
        as if it is the last
                words my voice
                        will ever utter

    I AM BEAUTIFUL

There's dancing
In the belly all day long
Constant restlessness
Outgrowing myself
My skin doesn't like it
There are growth marks where my flesh fought
Against its own expansion
My belly is never settled
Always indecisive
Second guessing its own potential
There's a waterfall of breath
Waiting to calm
Over the ache
The buoy in my chest
Begs me to exhale
Seasick with worry and wavering

How do I tell myself it's okay to just let go?

To trust the universe and my intuition
I'm growing
I'm growing
Come on self
Keep up

Future soil
       drifts from trees
              in the color pattern of sunset
Blanketing the streets in sweltering floods

This is the weather that craves the comfort
              of another body's embrace

Make me warm

Make me forget that day is darkening before its time

Hold me like there is no tomorrow

Better yet
Hold me like summer solstice

Pretend we are school kids
       with only oceans
             on our minds

The wind is whirling outside our window
It's the whizzing

of the popped open fire
hydrant in my daydream

The trees are nearly naked
necking my lawn
Heavy from yesterday's rain

There is no need for us to leave
the ease
of this couch

Outside is a heat wave of wind
And I'd much rather make love

Things us kids pressed
On the dark face
Before it hardened
Pale
Remembering delicate old injuries

The spines of names and leaves

There

We are not forgotten

Not the children of lure and memories

My hands
        forever etched in stone

Someone will think of me
Child-like palms embedded into eternity

These are the ways we defy the gods

I will teach my children
How to stay young

How to create lasting impressions
Mold substance around our language creators
Let the leaves tell our stories
After we are gone
We will be reincarnated
New children piling leaves and plunging
Into imagination
Unused hope carriers
Letting the cement dry
After their palms are imprinted

One day we will be called fossils

Walking history

I leave pieces behind for them
I don't want my tradition to one day be extinct

I write it down
In the name of history
No detail is unexplained
My culture will not be forgotten
My journal
Our immortality
Keep the light on for me

Save me a designated place on the floor
I will be there
Late

But still on time

There is cutting to be done

Potatoes to be peeled

We will sleep with hunger in our bellies
Stuffing will fill the heavy air

Awaken to Macy's day parade blaring
Grandma still asleep on the couch

My family
Is a picture
Three generations
Telling stories and gossiping
                    of love life and good times

This is our
Holiday
Our culture

My poetry a time capsule

There are instructions
For when all that is left of me is a palm print

You cannot forget us

Smiles once found
        happiness on her face

It's been a while since they rested there
Prayed in hope that death not find comfort
                in her throat

Gathered no signs of being heard
Smiles can't find peace with the threat
             of death
             on tips
             of tongue

She walks slow now

Once pulled me to keep up with her

She used to cook me home fries
Arthritis dis-empowering her hands
Yet she peeled potatoes for me

We want her to peel potatoes for my nephew
Want her to find strength in his eyes
Bits of my brother are in him

My brother was a warrior

Grandma
       recharge your power
I want to electrify your soul
Chemo is making you fragile
Hold my hand
I want to force hope onto your palms
Get strength circulating through your body

Grandma
     we need you

      Let the phoenix
           that has died
           and lived in your
                belly
                fly up

Burning any bit of death that thought it had a home

I can't stand idle while small demons attack
       the voice that lulled me Christmas carols
So grandma
      I will write
This is the only thing I've ever known how to do

Will you take it?
Murmur it with hand on throat like an exorcist
Make that demonic disease decease
I know that power is in me
For sure it is in you
Us women are strong
I'm positive you have forgotten that
Hold on
Sunshine still shines
        often days

Grandma
        do you look?

Shine is good for the soul
Courage is embedded in sunsets
Please don't forget to look
Your blinds are always closed
Shutting him out won't stop him from coming
He's set in your grand children's eyes
We are staring at you
Tell me you feel a change
Yesterday you cooked dinner
Last week it was hard to walk

The gods and I have conversations

Most times one-sided but I suppose
      they are listening

I'm not sure if you are
Hum some Aretha if yes
I never thought I'd miss your country talk
Say anything loud and clear
I want to imitate you
I miss this
Have questions that are unanswered
Tell me of our history
Tell me the stories your momma told you
I want my children's bellies filled with knowledge
Garnish mine
Spin my mind with thoughts I never thought could
be birthed with conversation with you
Spin it like the baton you twirled and got stuck
      in the Christmas tree
There are far too many memories
      and conversations to create
I guess I'm begging you to hold on
One day when there's no highs but lows
Grandma
      remember me and this poem

Rest in Peace Grandma Cece, 2010

Make me smile
Mean really smile
Make my face hurt from showing teeth

This is a story of a daughter
A girl
Learning to be strong
Her mother young
Unprepared for her daughter's fight
Girl birthed two months too early
Not fully cooked in the oven
Womb clinching to hold her in
Ma not ready
Sat legs crossed in hospital bed

She know that's no way to birth a baby

Sister and Doctor
Both say
> *She coming*
> *Girl gone be born*
> *First day of Fall*

Head first
Head full of hair
Head strong
Ma must have had heart burn all pregnancy
Took three slaps to make her cry

Ma had no name for her yet
Came too early
Already stubborn and nameless
Ma's sister said name her Masada
Said something of fortress
And Hebrews fighting Romans
There the name settled
First time girl smiled
Felt important and necessary to be named
Was no easy task raising her
Her voice loud and clumsy
Said things kids shouldn't
Dreamt of being grown
Ma didn't know how to contain her
Daughter's wondrous spirit
Full of curiosity
Words and song

Ma did know how to calm her
Took her all up in her arms
Rocked her back and forth
Ease your mind

Words ain't going nowhere

Sometimes you just need to be

Sure

      to this day you can still see

Masada rocking
Feeling her Ma's love and seeking solitude

Bang

One day Ma wakes at 4am
Sits straight up in the bed
Drinks water to settle herself
Then finds rest

Masada's been preparing to be strong
Her clumsy mouth now home to power and song

Little girl far from being hushed
Her brother left this world at 4 am
                in search of better lands

Places where brown boys find work easy
No street corner pass offs

Dreaming is feasible
Seeing 25 possible
So many hope

He found that land
Finds comfort in the simplicity of everyday life

Masada's mom is broken now
She takes her Ma up in her arms
Trying to rock her steady to calmness

grandma has gone to see the heavens
wonder if she's seen my brother

Afterword

He was 23 years old when he was taken from us. It was May, four months before my 20th birthday, and he was gone—killed—in our hometown.

My family is close. The type that hugs, and says *I love you* before bed, work, and the end of every phone call. My parents taught us this, wanting each other to know that the love is real, and time is not often on our side. After he, Andre, passed we had to relearn to breathe, relearn the sound of our own voices, and remind ourselves that it takes thriving to be the ones that remain.

Writing and performing proved to be the coping tool that I needed. It also provided the opportunity to begin investing in my community by co-founding FreeVerse! with some of my closest friends. After Andre passed I made a conscious decision to be happy, and not be overcome by my family's tragedy. If poetry did not offer me the catharsis that I needed, I'm not sure where I'd be. So, here's a book—it is filled with so many emotions; some are well thought out while others

are urgent and raw. But mainly, it contains so much of my heart.

After performing for a few years in a spoken word trio, Lyricist In Full Emancipation (LIFE), my friends and group mates, decided young people in our city needed to be exposed to this empowering art form. We founded FreeVerse! to nurture and invest in spoken word and performance with youth in the city of Lowell in the summer of 2009.

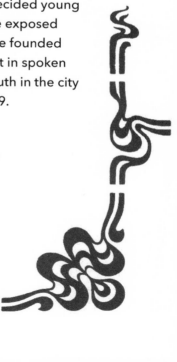